GUIDE

# SURVIVING PROM

TAYLOR MORRIS

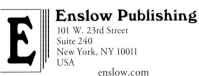

**Enslow Publishing**
101 W. 23rd Street
Suite 240
New York, NY 10011
USA
enslow.com

Published in 2018 by Enslow Publishing, LLC.
101 W. 23rd Street, Suite 240, New York, NY 10011

**Library of Congress Cataloging-in-Publication Data**

Names: Morris, Taylor.
Title: Surviving prom / by Taylor Morris.
Description: New York: Enslow Publishing, 2018. | Series: Teen survival guide | Includes bibliographical references and index. | Audience: Grades 7-12.
Identifiers: LCCN 2017016835| ISBN 9780766091894 (library bound) | ISBN 9780766093577 (pbk.) | ISBN 9780766093584 (6 pack)
Subjects:  LCSH: Proms—Handbooks, manuals, etc.
Classification: LCC GV1746 .M67 2018 | DDC 793.3/808837318—dc23
LC record available at https://lccn.loc.gov/2017016835

Printed in the United States of America

**To Our Readers:** We have done our best to make sure all websites in this book were active and appropriate when we went to press. However, the author and the publisher have no control over and assume no liability for the material available on those websites or on any websites they may link to. Any comments or suggestions can be sent by email to customerservice@enslow.com.

**Photo Credits:** Cover Monkey Business Images/Shutterstock.com; p. 5 Hill Street Studios /Blend Images/Getty Images; p. 9 @erics/Shutterstock.com; pp. 11, 35 Jupiterimages /Photolibrary/Getty Images; p. 12 JGI/Jamie Grill/Blend Images/Getty Images; p. 15 Ariwasabi/Shutterstock.com; p. 19 George Doyle/Stockbyte/Getty Images; p. 23 Peter Seyfferth/imageBROKER/Getty Images; p. 27 Tim Hall/Cultura/Getty Images; p.31 Image Source/Getty Images; p. 32 Brian Chase/Shutterstock.com; p. 33 Digital Vision/Photodisc /Getty Images; p. 36 Blend Images - Hill Street Studios/Brand X Pictures/Getty Images; p. 38 Verity Jane Smith/Stockbyte/Getty Images; p. 43 kali9/E+/Getty Images; cover and interior pages graphic elements © iStockphoto.com/marigold_88 (waves), Milos Djapovic/ Shutterstock.com (rough texture), Miloje/Shutterstock.com (circles).

# CONTENTS

# INTRODUCTION

You've been daydreaming about it for months. (Or maybe dreading it?) Prom. Your big chance to pull out all the stops and go full-out formal. You've watched movies with elegant prom or formal dance scenes and have wondered what your own night will be like. A *Carrie* horror show (2013 or 1976, take your pick) or an unstoppable party à la *Footloose* (2011 or 1984)? The possibilities for what can happen on a night filled with glittering faux jewels, dresses down to there, sky-high heels, and elegant tuxedos are totally endless, limited only by what your imagination can conjure up.

So what is *prom*?

Prom is a high school tradition that culminates (typically) in the end of your high school days, or at least the end of the school year. It's as much a part of American high schools as Friday night football, SATs, and pop quizzes. It's fancy dresses, rented tuxedos, limos, awkward photos, and all-night parties. It's fun, it's torturous, it's the best night of the year. It's a night out with your friends to dance and laugh and celebrate surviving high school. It's a night you will remember for the rest of your life—good or bad.

It may also be the most glam night of your life up to now. Prom means dressing like you're headed to the Oscars,

Get ready for a great night of friends, flirting, and fun! Prom night is here!

hanging out with all your best friends, and, a lot of times, saying goodbye to high school. It's even a little bit about saying goodbye to your childhood. If you head to prom as a senior, college and real-life stuff is just a few summer months away. But at prom, it's all about friends and fun in fancy clothes.

Prom is what you make of it. Expectations can run incredibly high; we advise you try to keep it reasonable. Don't call it the best night of your life—call it the most glam night of your life *so far*. Prom is a rite of passage and we want you to make the most of it — without going nuts. So here we are with the answers to all your questions, from prep to post-party and everything in between. Let's get ready to dance the night away!

# CHAPTER ONE

# THE BUILDUP

## THE ASK: CREATIVE PROMPOSALS AND WHERE TO FIND THEM

Thanks to social media, the pressure for splashy promposals—when asking a date to prom becomes an event that is Instagram, Snapchat, YouTube, and otherwise viral-ready—is at an all-time high. There are literally hundreds of creative ways to ask a date to prom and you can find them all online. Browse sites like Pinterest for ideas to steal or use as a springboard for your own take. Search #promposal on Instagram for even more concepts.

In planning out how to ask your date to the prom, think about:

- What his unique interests are
- What your shared interests are

- What she's obsessed with—anything from a particular candy or food to their favorite musician.
- A funny moment the two of you had

Tailor your promposal to what your date likes and is interested in. You can get inspiration online, but your hopeful date should see that the ask is all about him.

And if you'd rather go old-school and simply call up your date, or present her with a rose and ask her to go to prom with you? That's great too! Not everything has to be a social media event. (We swear.)

# WHO'S ASKING WHO?

If you're a girl and you plan on sitting around and waiting for the person you like to ask you to prom, we've got a little piece of advice for you: Get off your bum and go ask them yourself! Trust us, some social expectations are totally outdated! So take charge of your fate by beating him to the promposal. You can make it as elaborate, sweet, or low-key as he would. Same rules apply—if you go big, make sure you know his interests…and that he doesn't already have a date!

# OH, THE WAYS YOU CAN GO!

From head to toe and beginning to end, there are tons of decisions to be made for this one night. But who you're going with? This one is important.

Plan well and you can take your date's hand knowing a relaxed and fun night is in store.

You want the night to be as fun and stress-free as possible, right? Lots of people feel this way, which is why more and more proms see groups of friends attending together—some coupled up, some just hanging together as a team. What's best for you?

*Classic Date = you plus your date.* You're basically on a date. Just the two of you. You do dinner before, ride together, find your friends at the prom, and then head to the after-party together. Pro: possibility for a romantic-feeling night. Con: feeling isolated from your friends.

# AVOID BEING A PROMZILLA

promzilla: Noun
(plural: promzillas)
(usually humorous) *A teen who is exceptionally obsessed with preparing for his or her prom and ensuring it turns out the way envisioned.*

Planning and staying organized and on schedule are good things, but you might be a promzilla if:

- You begin planning in September…before you even have a date.
- You expect a viral-worthy ask and nothing less.
- Your friend is crying over a breakup, and you tell them they better find another date fast—prom is just 176 days away!
- You insist on choosing your date's clothes.
- You insist on color coordinating with your friends' dresses.
- Your budget is enough to run a small European country.
- Your outfit costs as much a wedding gown.
- Your day-of beauty prep puts Oscar contenders to shame.

It's great to care about prom and having a fancy, fun night, but be sure to keep it all in perspective. It's just one night — and you still want to have your friends—and some money!—in the morning.

*Date Plus Group = you, your date, and all your friends (and their dates).* This is by far the most popular way to prom. Everyone pairs up and then does the whole night together. Meet beforehand for pictures (of all twenty of you!), share a giant limo, sit at the same table, and head to the after-party together. The date situation here can be as low-key or intense as you want. You have the freedom to float between your date and your friends, have sweet moments together as a couple then go whip your hair on the dance floor with your crew.

Dance like you just don't care—because you're having too much fun! Prom is about the friends you've made—guys and girls, romantic and not—so let loose to your own beat.

*Solo … planned or not.* It can happen to anyone. Really. The night of prom is approaching and you suddenly find yourself without a date.

Maybe you made the decision that you don't want to spend the evening in some pseudo-romantic situation that you're just not feeling. Or maybe you get ghosted a week before prom.

Whether you walk through the door totally by yourself or go dateless with your group of paired-up friends,

You don't need to spend a ton of money to have a great night. Money won't buy memories, after all!

deciding to go to prom dateless is a big bold move that we fully support. (Hey, Andie *Pretty in Pink*-ed her way to the ballroom with her head held high.) Because honestly? Skipping the ritual of prom—especially senior year—could be something you'll always regret. Be brave and go for it. Because truthfully, once the party gets started, no one will even notice who came with whom.

# THE BUDGET

If only we didn't have to worry about money, right? But most of us do, so planning out expenses is key to making your prom dreams come true. Talk with your parents to see if they can pitch in. Ask your date what they can pay for (dinner beforehand?), what you'll pay for (prom tickets?), and what you'll split (the limo or party bus?).

# POSSIBLE EXPENSES

- Limo rental
- Dinner before (if not part of the prom event your school is having)
- Prom tickets
- Dress/tuxedo
- Corsage/boutonniere
- Accessories, including shoes and jewelry
- Beauty bonuses, such as pro hair, makeup, and/or nails

# CHAPTER TWO

# PREP FOR PERFECTION

## THE LOOK

Before the dress or tux hunt can begin, think about how you want to look. What sort of vibe do you want to give off (and remember for decades to come with the everlasting evidence of the photos)? (No pressure.)

A good rule of thumb: you want to look like the best version of yourself but you still want to look like *you*. If you're not a super girly-girl then don't feel like you have to wear a poufy skirt with lace trimmings. If you're a low-key guy maybe you don't go for the '70s-style ruffled shirt.

You might already have a clear sense of your personal style and know exactly the kind of look you want. You're already ahead of the game! For many of us, we're still figuring out what our personal style looks like. So what are the options? Let's look at the options.

# HEY, GIRL. WHAT'S YOUR STYLE?

The truth is, an entire book could be written about your prom dress. It may seem like the most important part of the entire prom…but we hope your date and having a good time with your friends are the true highlights of your night. Still, you'll probably put a lot of thought and care into finding the perfect outfit for the night.

If you're thinking of trying out a radical new look for prom night, remember — your friends and family already love you for who you are!

If you're looking for a really specific outfit, do your homework online ahead of time to figure out where you might find your dream ensemble — and start looking early. If you buy an outfit online you'll want to leave plenty of time for it to arrive…and get it altered or send it back if it doesn't fit well or look flattering.

There are lots of styles you can try out so let's break them down.

**Classic:** Clean lines and solid or subtle prints, classics are tried-and-true dress cuts from the past, like A-line skirts. They're modest and don't show too much skin. Classic *never* goes out of style.

**Modern:** For the girl who wants her look to be of the moment and on-trend. You can go super on-trend, belly-baring, perhaps? Or maybe you don't want to wear a dress at all. For some girls, a dress is equal to some forms of medieval torture. Consider rocking a femme tux. We've seen it all over the red carpets worn by some of Hollywood's top stars. The look can be both totally feminine and downright empowering—and together that equals sexy! To mix it up, instead of a stiff shirt buttoned to the neck, go for a feminine blouse with a loose black tie.

**Romantic:** Flowing, wavy, pale colors from white to rose pink or hazy sunshine yellow, this look could easily be topped with a flower crown.

**Vintage:** This look is retro, usually with a modern twist to keep it from looking like a costume. It references a specific time period, like flowing kaftans from the '70s, a full circle skirt from the '50s, fringe from the '20s, or finger-wave hair à la the 1930s. Consider hitting your mom's closet or a vintage store and then adding some modern accessories.

**Punk:** We're envisioning shredded black tulle, heavy eye makeup, fingerless lace gloves…and possibly a broken tiara? This is for the fringe girl who shirks trends and blasts her own path. Basically: rules not required.

**Princess:** The evil twin of punk, this look goes for sugary sweet and full of innocence. Princess-style dresses are often strapless with full flowing skirts in pastel colors with sequins galore. Keep your makeup simple and your hair elegant for this pretty-girl look.

*Rent, borrow, or buy?*

**Rent**

Renting is a great option. There are sites that loan high-end designer dresses and take care to make sure the dress fits by sending you two sizes. Renting is a great way to save money while looking like a million bucks.

*Pros:* Red carpet–ready dress

*Cons:* Your dress arrives just a day or two ahead of prom, and it'll be the first time you've put it on and can match it up with all the accessories you might have already bought. And if it looks bad or the fit isn't quite right? You are out of luck.

### Borrow

If you have an older sibling, cousin, or friend who's the same size, borrowing your prom dress could be the way to go. It's another way to save money but unlike renting, you can try it on well ahead of time to ensure a perfect fit.

*Pros:* Money saved on a dress that's new to you

*Cons:* You may have to let go of your perfect dress in favor of the perfectly priced dress (aka free!).

### Buy

You get exactly what you want (within your budget, of course) and can maybe even wear it again someday (your first sorority formal, perhaps?). Plus you can get something that's new this season, as opposed to a dress that's *so* two years ago—if you care about that sort of thing.

*Pros:* It's yours, all yours!

*Cons:* This one will hit your wallet the hardest—especially if you have expensive taste.

# HEY, BOY. YOU'RE MORE THAN A PENGUIN.

Whoever said all tuxedos look the same hasn't watched a Hollywood red carpet event in years. Tuxedos can be as varied as its wearer's personality. Vest or cummerbund, black and white or something with color, a suit fit, a real bowtie… there are lots of options for you to stand out in the black-and-white crowd—more than you bargained for, in fact. Did you know that according to Buzzfeed and Pinterest, there

Menswear has upped its game, so you have a lot of choices to make. Be sure to pick the look that makes you feel most like yourself.

are at least ten different kinds of collars, six types of cuffs, and three styles of vests? And you thought this would be simple!

## SO MANY STYLES

"Tuxedo" refers to a jacket-and-pants combo, typically black, where the jacket has satin lapels and the pants have a satin stripe down the outer side of the leg. But even that definition is up for wild interpretation. Here are just a few ways to make your tux stand out.

- Subtle colors like burgundy, charcoal gray, or navy take your tux from standard to outstanding. Dark colors keep it classy and elegant; wear light, bright colors (sherbet orange, anyone?) and suddenly you're Lloyd Christmas (which is awesome — so long as that's the look you're going for).

- The white dinner jacket is elegant and oh-so Bond. Worn with black pants and shoes, this look ensures you'll look classically handsome.
- Colored or framed lapels give a standard look some extra pizzazz. A white jacket with black-framed lapels gives you subtle pop while keeping it classy.
- Wearing a straight tie instead of a bowtie is something lots of men do to keep the tux look fresh. This doesn't mean you can pull out the suit you wore to your second cousin's wedding, and slap a cummerbund on it and call it formal wear. The only difference is the black satin tie. The rest of the tuxedo parts stay the same.
- Tails make for the most dramatic of the tuxes. Want to make sure you're noticed? This may be the way to go. Traditionally, tux tails are when the jacket is short

# ANATOMY OF A TUXEDO

- Jacket
- Pants
- Bowtie
- Vest

- Dress shirt
- Cufflinks
- Dress shoes

in the front (hits at about your waist) and long in the back, down to the back of your knees and split down the center.

# THE PERFECT FIT

For most guys, renting the suit is the only way to go. Few high schoolers own a tuxedo. This is good news for you, since you're spending far less money than a girl who chose to buy a dress. Even better, the folks at the rental shop will help you find the perfect fit. Here's what a good shop should make sure of:

- Shirtsleeve length should hit right at the base of your wrist.
- Shirt body should be slim and not too bunchy.
- The shoulder seams need to hit right at the intersection of your shoulder and bicep.
- Your collar shouldn't choke you, but it also shouldn't look like you're wearing your dad's shirt. It should be just wide enough to fit two fingers snugly.
- Your pants should "break" in the proper place—the crease your pants make down toward your ankle need to land in the right spot. Bring your dress shoes to the fitting for this very reason. Otherwise you might end up with pants too long and dragging at the heel.
- Your suit jacket should cover your bum, but the sleeves should not cover your shirt cuffs entirely.

# GETTING TIED UP

If you decide clip-on bowties are for little boys and want to wear a classic bow tie, may we suggest some practice to make perfect? Pull up a YouTube video and get to work in the days ahead of prom to figure out how to tie it with ease. Watching a video in the back of the limo on your way to dinner isn't a cute look and distracts from your date.

# LET'S GO SHOPPING!

Shopping can be fun…and exhausting. There should be a method and no madness to your hunt for the perfect outfit and, luckily, we have some ideas that will save you time, aggravation, and buyer's remorse.

1. Research ahead of time. Know what styles you want to try on before you head out the door. Check out magazines, your favorite blogs, and more for ideas.
2. Know which stores in town sell the kind of outfit you're looking for. Look online at their inventory (but know that it won't be a complete representation of in-store options).
3. Give yourself time. Not just far enough ahead of prom (we recommend two to three months), but plenty of time at the store, too. You'll want to really browse and

Bring along a relative or your most trustworthy friend for your prom shopping trip. You'll have fun—and find a killer outfit.

try on lots of options, even styles you *think* you're not into.

4. Bring shoes with the heel height you'll want to rock on prom night. They likely won't be the shoes you'll wear, but you'll want to see how the full-length dress looks and how it skims the ground, or what length your tux pants need to be hemmed to.

5. Snap a pic—if the store manager doesn't mind. It's the best way to keep track of the top picks of the day and get a good visual on how it fits and looks on you.

6. To make changing easy, wear a pullover shirt and slip-on shoes or boots.

7. Bring along someone whose opinion you trust. Parent, sibling, best friend: someone who is honest and kind and won't steer you wrong.

8. Finally, make sure that your dream outfit stands up to any dress codes your school might be enforcing. You don't want to spend all this time and money putting together your look only to be turned away at the door. (Though, frankly, we hope your school doesn't have any dated rules of dress and lets you express your style and personality as you see fit!)

# COLOR COORDINATE WITH YOUR DATE?

Look, you don't have to be all matchy-matchy with your date but you might want to look like you came together. Let your date know what color you're wearing, and see if he or she wants to dress in a complementary color. Or, if you don't want your date to see your outfit until prom, send an extreme close-up pic of your dress, tux, or cummerbund so he or she can show the color to the florist for your corsage or boutonniere.

Girls, make sure your date knows if you prefer a wrist or pin-on corsage. If you're wearing a strapless dress you'll probably want to avoid trying to pin anything to your dress—you don't want the flowers weighing down your top. (Lots of girls find wrist corsages easier to wear and more comfortable.)

Whatever you do, don't try to dictate what your date wears. This is his night too, and if he's wearing an orange tuxedo — good for him! You guys will get lots of attention. Just imagine how you'd feel if someone tried to tell *you* what to wear?

# CHAPTER THREE

# THE FINAL COUNTDOWN

## NIGHT-BEFORE SLEEPOVER

It's almost time! High school is as much about the friendships you've made as the stuff you've learned (just don't tell the teachers we said that). To help make prom super special, have a sleepover the night before the big night. Watch old movies with great prom scenes (*10 Things I Hate About You*, *Never Been Kissed*, *Mean Girls*). You can help each other get ready (do each other's nails, test out applying fake lashes, try alternative hairstyles). Guys, it's your party too. Get your bros together for some fun.

Just don't overdo it before it all begins. Everyone should get a good night's sleep even if you all crash together. The day of the prom, avoid any major day-long commitments, as well as sunburn. We don't want you showing up on prom night red and exhausted. Try to keep your lead-up to the night as chill

Pre-pre-party! Start the fun early by gathering your besties for a sleepover. But don't skimp on the beauty sleep—tomrrow is the real all-nighter.

as possible. The last thing you want is to be yawning before you've even had your first dance.

## GETTING READY

First piece of advice: test everything before the big night. Never had a spray tan? Don't try it the day of the prom. Figure it's time you started wearing five-inch heels? Not tonight, you won't. (Really. Check out our section on shoes.) Always wanted to be a platinum blond? Maybe not right before the one night of your life that you'll take fourteen thousand more photos of yourself than usual.

Since prom is very much about glam and beauty and looking your stunning best, we have some tips and reminders on how to make sure you look back on all those photos in twenty years without cringing.

# YOUR PRE-PROM PREP

- Make sure you have your date secured!
- Buy tickets.
- Order your date's boutonniere or corsage —and don't forget to pick it up.
- Pick up your outfit — dress, tux, or otherwise.
- Don't forget all the accessories—shoes, clutch, jewelry.
- Make hair/makeup/nail appointments if necessary.
- If you get a limo call the company to confirm that it's going to actually show up. Make sure it's a reputable company, and keep all email correspondences you've had with them…just in case.
- Stay healthy—eat well, drink water, exercise, take multivitamins, keep up your beauty routine (especially skin).
- Stay in line—don't get yourself grounded a week before prom.

*Hair*

Having a pro do your hair? Make the appointment weeks in advance—up to two months, even—to make sure you get the day and time you want. Take a picture of what you want your stylist to achieve so there's no confusion. Take a picture of your dress to discuss a look that will complement your dress, from a sophisticated chignon to a whimsical braid.

For those of us who need a more budget-friendly option—got a friend who happens to be a whiz with hair? Someone who can do red-carpet waves or a sleek side fishtail? Ask if she'll help you with your hair. Offer to pay her a small fee or trade off for a big favor.

There's the obvious and most cost-saving way to do your hair—by yourself. To make it look extra-special, choose a style online or in magazines and practice in the weeks leading up to prom. YouTube has hair (and beauty) tutorials galore, so your main problem will be narrowing the videos down to a few. Lots of practice will ensure your hair *do* isn't a hair *don't* come prom night.

*Nails*

The salons will likely be flooded the day before or day of prom, so if you can make an appointment beforehand, do it! It certainly can't hurt. If you're getting a pedicure make sure you give your toes plenty of time to dry *fully and completely* before putting on your shoes. Getting your nails done the day before will ensure no shoe smudging.

Make sure your nail color nicely complements your dress color and style. Even consider doing an easy, neutral shade. Check out Hollywood red-carpet fingers to see what looks best.

If you want to snazz it up with nail art and can't afford the high-end salons that literally make art out of your fingertips, try your local drugstore. There are tons of easy gel kits and appliqués, not to mention YouTube tutorials on how to get the latest nail trends for far less money. (Seems like a perfect sleepover activity, too!)

# THE TAKE–WITH ESSENTIALS

What to pack in your tiny little purse:

- Lip color/gloss
- Your phone, because obviously
- ID
- Debit or credit card for emergencies and cash for the same reason
- Mints
- Bobby pins or any (small) hair fix-it tool
- Strips of moleskin, in case of blisters
- Double-sided apparel tape

# THAT (FAKE) GOLDEN GLOW

A word of warning: when you're first sprayed with a tan in a can, the color can look ashy. Also, be prepared: the spray

Primp and prep for extra pop, just don't go over the top! And be sure to test everything before the big day.

smells a bit funny. Both will go away once you shower (usually twelve hours afterward) but until then you're stuck. If you're going for a spray tan, do it two to three days in advance of prom to get that sun-kissed glow.

## GENTLEMEN'S TO DOS

It may seem like girls have a lot more prep to take care of right before prom, but you've got a check list, too!

31

Pretty flowers add a personal and romantic touch to your night—and they smell amazing, too.

- A week before prom, make sure your tux is ready to go — that means pressed and cleaned. Also make sure the florist has your corsage order ready (you *did* order a corsage, right?).
- On the day of, do the full shower and shave. Got your shoes polished and clean socks?
- When you leave for the night, make sure you have cash, a loaded debit card, fully charged phone with a car service app ready to go in case you need a safe, sober driver. Oh, the corsage. Don't forget the corsage!

Believe it or not, your prom is a huge deal for your parents, too! Humor them and smile for their hundreds of photos. They'll appreciate it!

# PRE-PROM PARTY

This is something lots of parents love to help plan…and maybe sort of take over. Let them! A pre-prom party can be as much for the parents as it is for you and your friends, so give them that hour or so to fuss over you and (maybe slightly) annoy you by taking hundreds of posed photos. You'll be rid of them soon enough once you graduate, and you'll totally appreciate all the photos they're taking of you, your date, and your friends.

33

# CHAPTER FOUR

# THE MOMENT HAS ARRIVED

Months of preparation, saving money, stressing, shopping, sampling, and agonizing have finally culminated in tonight—*the* night. If you did a good job planning there should be nothing left to do but have a great time. Remember: this is what it all leads up to. You are at *the prom*. Enjoy yourself!

Just like there are pressures every day at school and on weekends, you're going to feel them on prom night—maybe more so than normal. So here's our guide to surviving some pitfalls of prom—while still looking fabulous and feeling strong.

## DRINKING ... NOT JUST SODA

A topic surprising to no teen ever, there is drinking (aka alcohol) at prom…before prom…and after prom. It's illegal, but it happens. So: how to deal?

Let's say you're not into drinking and have no plans to do so on prom or any other night. First off, your parents are thrilled and probably want to hug and thank you for being

It's time to reap the rewards of all your planning. Our best advice? Just have fun!

so responsible. However, what if your friends *do* plan on drinking? There might be champagne at the very least because *hello*, it's a celebration and a party and everyone is having *just one glass*. (And maybe there's some whiskey hidden in the trunk along with a case of beer because come on—*prom*!) It's awkward, we know. You probably don't want to come off as holier-than-thou and full of judgment but you also don't want to do something you really don't want to do. (And we think you're awesome for sticking by your convictions.) So how do you handle it? It depends on your personality.

- If you're the kind of person who truly doesn't care what others think, a casual "No, thanks" will work. But admittedly, not all of us are that smooth and full of confidence.Come up with something ahead of time

You're practically an adult, so it's time to start acting that way. Being responsible and saying no to alcohol is a great way to start. You can still have fun sober, so don't let anyone tell you otherwise.

(like maybe you're taking antibiotics or some other medication that can't be combined with alcohol) so that you're not fumbling in the moment.

- Try being vague. "Maybe later" or "I don't feel like it right now" can help thwart attention. Blame it on something you (maybe) have to do tomorrow. "I would but I've got my grandparents coming in town tomorrow and can't be all hungover."
- Be the hero by designating yourself the token sober person for the night. Tell your friends you can help watch out for adults looking to ruin prom by busting them for alcohol or be the designated driver.

We know getting pressured is hard, especially by your own friends who you love and care about. Still, it happens, and we admire you for standing strong.

But what if you do plan on drinking? Drinking lowers your inhibitions. That's the first thing you should know. And then, all else can follow:

- **Fights.** It's true. You're more likely to brawl if you're feeling invincible and irrational thanks to all that cinnamon whiskey.
- **Crying fits.** Emotions can become heightened when boozing. Get ready to have your makeup ruined or be potentially caught on someone's phone saying "I love you, man" a lot.

If your date really likes you, they'll respect the boundaries you set. You and only you can decide how far you want to go.

- **Unprotected sex.** Being drunk can mean getting sloppy about stuff like safety and responsibility.
- **Sexual assault.** Most girls know their assaulter, and alcohol is usually involved.

- **Blackouts and brownouts**, which is forgetting everything, or most parts of the night. Great way to make memories, huh?
- **Car accidents.** Really. According to the CDC, the leading cause of death in teens aged sixteen to nineteen is car crashes. And one in five of those fatal crashes involved alcohol.

Look, we're not trying to scare you. We just want you to know the risks. So if you do plan to drink, do it in a safe environment, never leave your drink unattended, hydrate with water before and after — and absolutely, positively do not drive or get in a car with anyone who has been drinking.

# DEALING WITH YOUR DATE'S (S)EXPECTATIONS

This is another biggie. Many teens seem to think prom night—with its very grown-up, sophisticated feel—is the perfect time to have sex or lose their virginity. What if you expect one thing to happen on prom night and your date expects something else?

"[Thinking about sex and expectations] should be part of prom prep," says Jeana M. Hill, MS, MFT, who works with kids, teens, and families. "The teen should know where their stopping point is and let their date know. Especially if they really like the person and would like to continue seeing them."

It can be a terrifying conversation—we get that. But as awkward as it is to bring up, setting boundaries beforehand will reduce chances of going further than you want and then being resentful that you felt pressured to go beyond your comfort zone.

If you're both comfortable with having sex, being open about it ahead of time will also allow you to prepare with protection—and avoid having a memory of prom night that you'll be taking care of for the next eighteen years.

If things go farther than you wanted, you need to tell an adult. Immediately. No excuses. Whatever happened, you aren't to blame, and you need to take action to protect yourself ASAP.

# AWKWARD...

What happens if there's someone else at the prom in the same dress — or "unique" tux — as you?
- Take a pic with them.
- Realize you both have great style and taste.
- The two of you are probably the only ones who notice or care so don't stress.
- Keep calm and party on.

# POST PROM

The after-prom party is a long-held tradition for late-night fun. It usually involves a pass to stay out all night, and what happens between the last song at the prom to first sunlight can vary pretty wildly. Here are some of the ways you can expect to spend the night.

## SCHOOL-SPONSORED PARTY

Many schools, prompted by hotel room debauchery and generally unsafe (and even deadly) events, now host chaperoned, all-night after-parties. Most are themed and all are alcohol free. They can be a fun way to party with your friends, stay out all night, and not have to worry about lying to your parents about where you are and what you're doing. Over the years, teachers, administrators, and parents have worked hard to keep the party from being lame and embarrassing to attend. Everything from casino games to go-carts and climbing walls can be found at these after-parties, so definitely give the good, clean fun a shot. You might actually enjoy yourself.

## HOTEL (ROOM) PARTY

First, you have to be at least eighteen to even rent a room, and you'll need a credit card with the same name for the deposit and incidentals on the room (like the mini bar and repairs if the room gets trashed). Still, many hotels aren't too keen to even allow teenagers to check into their rooms without an adult present, and they can say no the moment they see you. Teenagers, frankly, are a liability to them. They know you're not just watching HBO up there.

But maybe you get past all that and are able to secure a room with your date and friends. And then your friends' friends arrive. And then more. And before you know it, the cops are there. If there's alcohol in the room you can all be liable and get in legal trouble. The punishments range from a ticket to revocation of your driver's license, depending on the state you live in. (All of which could potentially be bad news for that college acceptance you're so pumped about.)

We get the advantages of a hotel party—you've got a safe place to stay for the night with no need to venture outside. You're off the streets. And that is good. But are you being honest with your parents about who is staying in the room and what you'll be doing? Will they know you got a room at all? There's still graduation to think about—you don't want to get grounded for all that fun!

## CRUISE AND FIGURE IT OUT

Your plan is to have no plans—just drive around from party to hotel to friends' houses, social butterflying your way around town. Frankly, this is the riskiest of all the after-prom possibilities. You might not be drinking, because we

# ADVICE FROM THE FRONT LINES

"Have FUN. This is a moment you'll always remember."

"Dance with a guy or girl no one else will dance with."

"It may be a great night but it's unlikely to be the best night of your life. Lighten up, don't put too much pressure on the prom or yourself, and have fun."

"Buy a dress you can wear again."

"Go in groups! No need to feel pressure to have a date."

We hope you have an amazing night with your friends, make a ton of new memories, take a million pictures, and get ready to move onto the next phase of your life. Congrats!

know you would never drink and drive or get in the car with someone who was drunk, right? But unfortunately others on the road might not be as mature as you. We're talking your fellow friends or other people at school. Plan a place to go post-prom ahead of time and stay there, or ask your parents to host a low-key movie night for all your friends. The key is to have fun but be safe and responsible.

# HAVE FUN!

Prom night really is an exceptional night. It might be an old-fashioned tradition, but we hope that when the night is over you'll have a lifetime of memories (and tons of great pics) to remember it all by. You'll have many more great nights in your life, but your high school prom will likely always hold a special place in your heart.

# GLOSSARY

**A-line** Describes a garment with a flared bottom and a tighter top, usually a dress or skirt.

**buyer's remorse** The feeling you get when you purchase something and then regret it later, often an expensive item.

**culminate** To get to the point you were working toward, a conclusion.

**cummerbund** A wide waistband sometimes worn with a tuxedo in place of a vest. Usually available in a variety of colors, which can be matched to others in a group (such as at a wedding) or a date's dress.

**debauchery** Extreme behavior, usually related to sex, alcohol, and drugs.

**incidental** A minor expense, in addition to the primary amount. At a hotel, these include fees for food, beverages, parking, and more.

**inhibition** A force inside you that keeps you from doing something, often expressing thoughts or desires.

**inventory** A total list of items available.

**liability** Something seen as a disadvantage.

**preemptive** Describes taking action before others can.

**pseudo** Fake or not real.

**revocation** The act of taking something back.

**rite of passage** A ritual, often cultural, that is associated with a life change, such as a graduation or wedding.

**torturous** Causing a lot of pain or torment.

**vintage** Representing a very nice or quality item from the past.

## BOOKS

Anderson, Daniel, and Jacquelyn Anderson. *The 10 Myths of Teen Dating: Truths Your Daughter Needs to Know to Date Smart, Avoid Disaster, and Protect Her Future*. Colorado Springs, CO: David C. Cook Books, 2016.

Chapman, Gary D., and Paige Haley Drygas. *A Teen's Guide to the 5 Love Languages: How to Understand Yourself and Improve All Your Relationships*. Bel Air, CA: Northfield Publishing, 2016.

Henderson, Elisabeth, and Nancy Armstrong. *100 Questions You'd Never Ask Your Parents: Straight Answers to Teens' Questions About Sex, Sexuality and Health*. New York, NY: Roaring Brook Press, 2013.

Schab, Lisa M. *The Self-Esteem Workbook for Teens: Activities to Help You Build Confidence and Achieve Your Goals*. Oakland, CA: New Harbinger Publications, 2013.

# WEBSITES

### It's Your Sex Life

*www.itsyoursexlife.org*

Straight, unfiltered answers to all your questions.

### Seventeen

*www.seventeen.com*

A girls' guide to dating, fashion, health, and surviving the teen years.

### Teens Health

*http://kidshealth.org/en/teens*

A safe, private place for teens who need honest, accurate information and advice about health, emotions, and life.

# INDEX